Contents

Early Signaling Systems

This semaphore stands in the German port city of Cuxhaven. It shows wind force and wind direction.

For thousands of years, people have used different ways to send messages over long distances. Some **cultures,** such as Native Americans, used smoke signals. Some sent messages by banging on drums that could be heard from far away. Others used a kind of signaling called **semaphore** that usually used flags or lights. In semaphore, someone would stand on a hilltop and hold a flag in each hand. The person would move the flags into different positions that stood for letters. When lights were used, they were moved into different positions or flashed on and off. Whatever the method, it worked to send messages as long as the parties who were communicating agreed on the meaning of the signals.

In the late 1700s, one kind of semaphore became very popular in France. Towers were built on a series of hilltops, about five to ten miles (eight to sixteen kilometers) apart. Inside each tower were two telescopes and a place for someone to stand. The telescopes faced in opposite directions so the person inside the tower could read messages from the closest tower on either side. Each tower also had two "arms," or long pieces of wood, attached

Members of the U.S. Army Signal Corps show off for the camera on a semaphore tower during World War I.

When Paul Revere made his famous ride in 1775 to warn the people of Lexington, Massachusetts, that the British were on their way, the signal that told how the troops would come—by land or sea—was a kind of semaphore. One lantern would be set in a church tower if the British were coming by land, or two if they were coming by sea.

to the top. The arms could move in different positions that stood for different letters. Each tower operator would signal the message to the next operator, and so on. Soon these towers were built all over Europe.

Another similar kind of signaling system used in the 1700s had shutters instead of arms. Six shutters, like doors, were opened and closed in different combinations. Each combination stood for a letter. This system was used in England and in the United States.

While this system was very helpful in passing information along quickly and at great distances, there were some drawbacks. For example, messages could not be sent at night, as the towers could not be seen. Bad weather could make it difficult to read the messages correctly. Also, messages could not be sent in secrecy: once a person knew how to read the arms, they would always know what the messages said. Finally, because the messages had to travel through so many different stations to get to their final destination, it was possible for more and more errors to creep in. Sometimes the message received at the final station was not the message that had originally been sent.

Early Experiments With Electricity

When you want to send someone a message, you might sit down at your computer, log on to the Internet, and write a quick e-mail. In just a few seconds, the person on the other end can be reading your message. Or you might pick up the telephone, dial a few numbers, and talk to your friend on the other end of the line.

Have you ever wondered how that all started? Do you know why you are now able to send messages through wires?

The power of electricity was discovered in the 1700s. Scientists during that century were able to use special containers that collected electric charges. Then they did experiments that showed that electricity

Today's communication **technology** began with the idea of using electricity to send messages through wires.

Early experiments with electricity led to the e-mail and instant messages that we are able to send today.

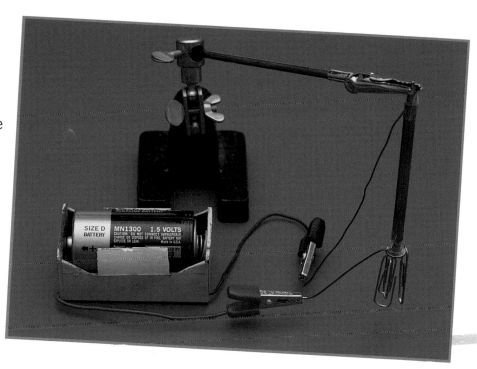

This electromagnet uses the energy from a battery to turn coiled wire into a magnet. The magnet attracts metal, like these paper clips.

could flow along wires. Sometimes they asked people to hold one end of a wire while they connected the other end of the wire to a **battery.** The scientists knew the power traveled through the wire because the people holding the wire would get a shock and say "ouch!" Their experiments showed that when the battery was on, electricity flowed. When the battery was off, the flow of **electric current** stopped. Then they tried hooking up the batteries to longer and longer pieces of wire to see how far the electric power would travel.

In the early 1800s, scientists discovered that electricity could turn a **coiled** wire into a **magnet** while the electric current was on. When the electricity was turned off, the wire was no longer a magnet. This kind of **magnetism** that can be turned off and on is different from that of a regular magnet. The kind of magnet that is made by electricity is called an **electromagnet,** and it is made into a magnet by **electromagnetism.** An American scientist named Joseph Henry worked with electromagnetism and made a simple machine that could send signals over a wire for more than a mile. Scientists knew these exciting discoveries would soon lead to something big.

Samuel F. B. Morse

Samuel Finley Breese Morse was born in Charlestown, Massachusetts, in 1791. He graduated from Yale University in 1810, then he traveled to London, England, to study art.

When his money ran out in 1815, Morse returned to the United States and began to paint **portraits** of wealthy people. He also enjoyed painting historical scenes, and he hoped to be chosen to paint historical **murals** inside the rotunda of the Capitol in Washington, D.C. But when someone else was chosen to do the murals, Morse turned away from art and began working on an idea that had come to him in 1832. His idea was to make an electric machine, something that would send messages through wires using electricity.

Not a lot was known about electricity in those days. In about 1800, Alessandro Volta invented the **voltaic cell,** a **battery** that stored electricity.

In 1820, Danish scientist Hans Christian Oersted found that electricity flowing through **coiled** wires created a **magnetic field.** Scientists called this property **electromagnetism.** When the **electric current** was on, the coil became magnetized. When the current was off, the **magnetism** stopped.

Scientists began to wonder if they could use electricity to send messages from one place to another. At first, they could send the electricity over only short lengths of wire.

Samuel Morse got the idea for sending messages using electricity and wire during a conversation he had on board a ship sailing from Europe to the United States.

This is one of Morse's paintings. It is a portrait of Mrs. Eliphat Terry.

Alfred Vail's father owned an ironworks, so it was easy for Vail to get metal parts to build telegraph instruments.

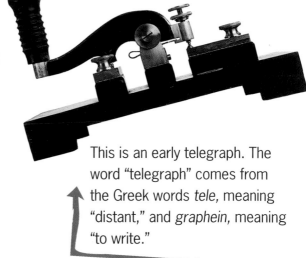

This is an early telegraph. The word "telegraph" comes from the Greek words *tele*, meaning "distant," and *graphein*, meaning "to write."

If the wire was too long, the flow of electricity became weaker and weaker. After much experimentation, they learned to send electricity through long wires.

At the same time, Morse worked on his **telegraph.** He was not a scientist, but he got help from **chemistry** professor Leonard Gale. Morse made a telegraph that sent a message over ten miles of wire that was coiled onto a wheel. Then another man, Alfred Vail, joined the team. Working together, they made a telegraph with a key that tapped out the message in code. An ink pen was attached to the machine. When the telegraph received a message, the pen would rise and fall to write the code, made up of dots and dashes.

Sir Charles Wheatstone and Sir William Cooke

While Morse was working in the U.S., Sir Charles Wheatstone and Sir William Cooke developed a telegraph in England. In 1837, at almost exactly the same time Morse completed his telegraph, they showed off their system. When electricity ran through its six wires, five pointers—like those on a compass—pointed to the letters that spelled out the message. In 1844, their telegraph was first used to announce the birth of Queen Victoria's son Alfred, and more people began to use it. By 1850, however, much of Europe decided to use Morse's system instead.

Sir Charles Wheatstone

Morse Code

In 1832, Samuel Morse had the beginnings of the idea for a good **telegraph code.** The code, he decided, would work best if made up of dots and dashes. With Vail's help, Morse perfected the code. The dots in the code stand for short bursts of electricity sent along the wires. The dashes stand for long bursts of electricity.

A	•—	N	—•	0	—————
B	—•••	O	———	1	•————
C	—•—•	P	•——•	2	••———
D	—••	Q	——•—	3	•••——
E	•	R	•—•	4	••••—
F	••—•	S	•••	5	•••••
G	——•	T	—	6	—••••
H	••••	U	••—	7	——•••
I	••	V	•••—	8	———••
J	•———	W	•——	9	————•
K	—•—	X	—••—	.	•—•—•—
L	•—••	Y	—•——	,	——••——
M	——	Z	——••	?	••——••

International Morse Code

The code on page 10 is called International **Morse code.** It developed over time in Europe, because the original Morse code—usually called American Morse code—used spaces as a necessary part of some letters, and this made it difficult to transmit properly over the radio. In 1865, most European countries voted to use International Morse code instead of American Morse code. International Morse code got rid of the spaces found in American Morse code. (See page 44 to compare American Morse code with International Morse code.)

American Morse code is considered the "old" code. It was what "landline" **telegraphers**—those who sent messages over wires on land—used in the United States. Messages that were not sent over land often used a differently coded system. For example, until recently, International Morse code was used by all ships worldwide.

There are a few differences between the two codes. The letter O in American Morse code, for example, is • •. The space between the two dots of the O lasts as long as a "dot" sound, usually called a "dit" by telegraphers. However, in International Morse code, O is tapped out — — —. Many people thought it was easier to tap out three characters in a row to make one letter than to tap out one, wait for a second, and tap out another. Also, they thought that the spaces or pauses between dots and dashes in letter signals would be confusing to the receiver.

People stopped using American Morse code when they stopped sending messages by telegraph. Today, "Morse code" almost always means International Morse code.

How the Telegraph Works

When you turn on something that runs on the power of electricity—your computer, for example, or a light—you open the **electric current.** When you turn the switch off, you stop the current. The electric current that gives power to the computer or the lamp runs through wires. You can think of the wires like streams. If someone blocks the stream, the water stops flowing. If someone removes the block, the water begins to flow again.

That's the basic idea behind how a **telegraph device** works. The switch on the device is called a **Morse key.** The key was made of brass or copper and could be raised or lowered. When the key was pushed, electricity flowed through the device. When it was released, the electricity stopped. During the years that the telegraph was used, many different kinds of keys were made. Some telegraph operators liked to use one kind of key, while other operators liked another kind.

Because buildings did not have wiring for electrical power during the early days of the telegraph, a **battery** was used to provide power for the device. In those days, batteries were made in glass jars. The combination of different chemicals inside the jars created electricity. Batteries could be hooked together to produce more power. The more batteries used to power the telegraph, the more power the device had.

The other main part of the telegraph device was the **electromagnet.** This was made from a **coil** of wire—usually copper wire, because electricity flows very well through copper. The wire was wound at least 50 times around

Know It

Charles Wheatstone also invented a device that punched holes in paper that matched what was being tapped out by the operator. When this paper was fed into a special machine, it could send messages ten to twenty times faster than a person could!

You can see the electromagnet—a thin wire wrapped many times around a spool—on this early telegraph device.

an iron spool. The wire became **magnetized** when electricity flowed through it. Once the wire became a **magnet,** it pulled on a piece of iron attached to it. In the early days of the telegraph, a pen or pencil was attached to the iron, and each "pull" made the pen write a dot or dash on a paper strip. Telegraph operators would tear off the strips of paper and **translate** the **Morse code** dashes and dots into words. By the 1850s, though, most telegraph operators preferred to just listen to the noises the iron's movement made instead of using machines that wrote down the dots and dashes. So devices called sounders were designed that would make a sound every time the iron was pulled. Each sound stood for a dot or a dash in Morse code. Operators listened to the sounds and could write down each word on a special **telegram** form.

When telegraph operators sent messages, they moved the device's key up and down. A short tap made the electricity stop for a short time, about as long as it takes you to say "dit." This was the sound that stood for a dot in Morse code. A long tap on the key stood for a dash, or "dah," in Morse code. The current flowed through a wire to other telegraph stations and made the telegraph devices there click for each dot or dash. Operators would listen for their own special signals, which let them know the message was for them. When an operator got a message, he or she would listen closely to the dots and dashes and write down the message. Another special signal told the operator that the message had ended.

What Hath God Wrought?

His invention of the telegraph made Samuel Morse very wealthy. In his old age, he donated money to educational institutions, religious organizations, and poor artists.

Morse, Gale, and Vail finally reached their goal of building a working **telegraph** and were ready to show it to the world. In 1838, the United States **Congress** wanted to build a telegraph system from New York to New Orleans. The system they planned to build was the one developed by Claude and Ignace Chappe, made of **semaphore** towers with movable arms. Congress asked for ideas, and Morse went to Washington, D.C., to show them his telegraph. At the time, though, Congress didn't agree that it was good enough to work.

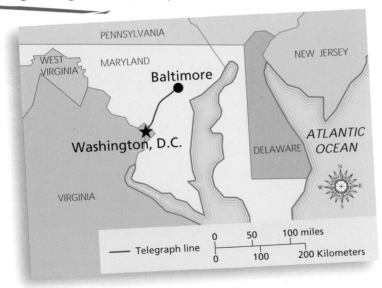

The first telegraph line built in the United States was only about 40 miles (64 kilometers) long. By 1850, there were about 12,000 miles (19,312 kilometers) of telegraph line all over the United States.

This sentence was written from Washington by me at the Baltimore Terminal

In 1842, Morse tried again. This time Congress voted to spend $30,000 on the telegraph. Not every member of Congress was sure the telegraph would work, but they were willing to give it a try.

Morse had telegraph lines put up between Washington, D.C., and Baltimore, Maryland, about 40 miles (64 kilometers) away. On May 24, 1844, he sent the first telegraph message on the line, using **Morse code** to tap out a quote from the Old Testament of the Bible: "What hath God wrought?" (The word "wrought" means made with a lot of effort.) The story goes that Morse told a young woman named Annie Ellsworth that she could come up with the message, because she was the person who had brought him the good news that Congress agreed to spend money on his telegraph line.

Even though the telegraph worked, few people were interested in it at first. Morse offered to let the U.S. government take over the system, but they didn't want it. So Morse got together with a man named Amos Kendall. Together, they found people to **invest** in their new company, called the **Magnetic** Telegraph Company. By autumn of 1845, the company was putting up telegraph lines between many cities in the Northeast.

This strip of paper came from the telegraph that received the first **telegram.** You can see the Morse code dots and dashes and Morse's handwriting below them.

mitted from Washington to Baltimore, and was indited by my much loved friend Annie G. Ellsworth. Sam'l F.B. Morse. Superintendent of Elec. Mag. Telegraphs.

The News Spreads

The first **telegraph** line strung between cities was built by Morse between Baltimore, Maryland, and Washington, D.C. Soon after Morse sent the first **telegram,** he found private **investors** to pay to have more wires put up. Then groups of businesspeople got together to form small telegraph companies. They would pool their money, put up telegraph wires, and charge people to send messages on their wires. Because these sets of wires were privately owned, it sometimes took a lot of work to get a message from one place to another. For example, Company A would send the message as far as its lines went. Then a person from Company A would have someone run the message down the road to Company B so that it could be sent on those lines. The farther a message went, the more companies had to be involved.

Three main telegraph companies soon emerged—the Western Union Telegraph Company, the New York & Mississippi Valley Printing Telegraph Company, and the American Telegraph Company—and they bought many of the smaller companies. This made it easier to send a message more directly from one city to another.

This telegram was sent from President Lincoln to General Grant on August 17, 1864. Telegrams made communicating during the civil war a lot easier.

Stagecoaches, like this one at a historic park in California, were the only way that many people could travel long distances in the United States during the 1800s. In one day, a typical stagecoach was on the road for about twelve to eighteen hours and covered only about 40 miles (60 kilometers) in good weather.

Telegraph lines went up all over the East Coast and west toward the Mississippi River. By 1848, there were about 2,000 miles (3,219 kilometers) of wire strung in the United States. By 1850, about 12,000 miles (19,312 kilometers) of wire were strung.

But one state, California, seemed to be out of luck. California became a state in 1850, but between it and the busy telegraph lines of the eastern half of the country were more than 1,000 miles (1,609 kilometers) of open land. Most of the land was divided into **territories** that belonged to the United States.

At first, stringing wire through the Mississippi River seemed to be a problem. But then scientists figured out how to make wire that would work underwater, and telegraph lines were sunk—first into the Mississippi, and then into the Missouri River. Everyone was convinced, though, that stringing wire across the plains, the steep Rocky Mountains, and the desert would be a big job.

Then, in 1861, civil war broke out between the states in the north and the states in the south. The northern states, called the Union, wanted California on their side. The people of California said that if they knew exactly what was going on, they might be able to help the Union. But news traveled slowly to California in those days. Even with the fastest stagecoach, it took about 23 days for mail to travel from St. Louis, Missouri, to California.

Wiring the West

Riders with the Pony Express took about ten days to travel the 1,800-mile (2,897-kilometer) route from St. Joseph, Missouri, to Sacramento, California.

In 1860, some thought the only way to get news from the eastern United States to the West was to send the mail with a good rider on a fast horse and tell them to go as fast as they could. This system, called the Pony Express, lasted for only nineteen months, from April 1860 to October 1861.

When the Civil War began in 1861, Californians were thirsty for news. California had been a state since 1850, but sometimes its people didn't feel that they were truly a part of the United States. Even the Pony Express brought news too slowly. California didn't know who was winning the war and where battles were being fought. If **Congress** passed a law or a new president was elected, Californians didn't hear about it for weeks.

Californians knew about the **telegraph**—there were even telegraph lines between several western cities—and they wanted their own link to the East. In 1861, Congress agreed. Western Union was chosen to put up lines from the nearest

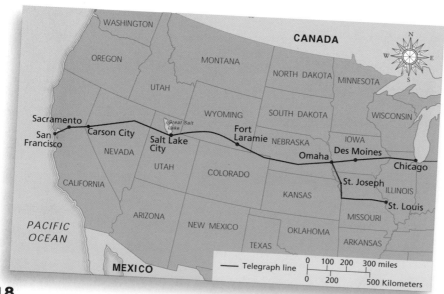

The transcontinental telegraph line was built in 1861 during the Civil War and linked the East with the West, making communication across the country almost immediate.

telegraph station in St. Joseph, Missouri, to California. Two crews of workers would build the line—one starting in the east, and one starting in the west. They would meet in Salt Lake City in Utah Territory.

It took hundreds of men to build the system. They formed wagon trains and moved slowly, covering about ten to twelve miles a day. They faced swarms of mosquitoes, thick mud, and deep rivers to cross. They never knew whether the local Native Americans would be friendly or hostile. Sometimes they went many miles out of their way looking for enough tall trees to serve as telegraph poles (they needed more than 42,000 in all!). They made deep holes in the ground and sunk the poles. Finally, they strung the wire, wrapping it in glass **insulators** at each pole.

Workers faced dangerous conditions putting up telegraph lines to the West— and not just climbing telegraph poles to attach the wire! They also had to cross the Rocky Mountains and the Sierra Nevada.

On October 18, 1861, the group that had worked from east to west reached Salt Lake City. Six days later, the westward-moving group arrived. The United States was wired!

Bison backscratchers

While the men from Western Union were busy putting up telegraph poles on the prairies, another group was busy knocking them down. Great herds of **bison** roamed the prairies in those days, and they didn't see many trees. Imagine their delight when they discovered that men had put up rows and rows of backscratchers for them! The bison crowded around the poles, taking turns rubbing their backs. After a while, all that rubbing caused the poles to tilt, then to fall over.

Western Union came up with a solution. They hammered sharp metal spikes into the poles. But the bison liked that even more. Now the poles were even better backscratchers, because the spikes poked through their thick hair and right onto their itchy skin! So the spikes were removed, and the workers just kept their eyes out for fallen poles.

Wiring the World

The **telegraph** was as popular in other countries as it was in the United States. In November 1851, the first major underwater **barrier** was crossed when cable was laid in the English Channel to connect England with France and the rest of the European continent.

Everyone agreed, though, that the biggest challenge was connecting the United States and Canada with Europe and Asia. It would be a huge job, because 2,500 miles (4,023 kilometers) of ocean stretched between North America and Europe.

This cross-section of the kind of undersea cable used in transatlantic telegraph lines shows a core of copper wires.

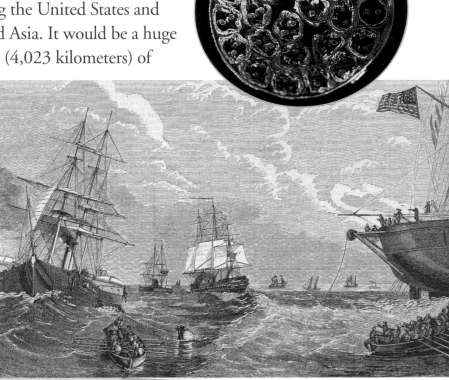

Ships met in the middle of the Atlantic Ocean to splice, or connect, the cable linking North America and Europe. Storms were so bad that one of the ships was almost wrecked.

It took several tries before telegraph cable was successfully laid across the Atlantic Ocean in 1866.

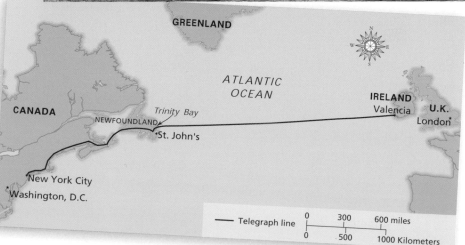

GREENLAND

ATLANTIC OCEAN

CANADA

NEWFOUNDLAND

Trinity Bay

St. John's

New York City

Washington, D.C.

IRELAND
Valencia

U.K.
London

—— Telegraph line

| 0 | 300 | 600 miles |
| 0 | 500 | 1000 Kilometers |

The plan was to lay cable between Ireland and Newfoundland, Canada, the closest point in North America. In 1857, a first attempt failed when the cable broke and fell into the Atlantic Ocean about 350 miles (563 kilometers) into the job. In 1858, the same group tried again. Two groups met in the middle of the Atlantic and connected the cable. Then one ship sailed east and one sailed west. The cable broke more than once and they had to start over, but by August 5, 1858, the link was completed.

The world celebrated with fireworks, parades, and more. But by September 1, the cable stopped working. Not until July 17, 1866, was another cable laid. Although everyone was cautious at first, this time it worked fine, and soon dots and dashes that started in London and Paris were **transmitted** into telegraph offices all over the United States and Canada.

Siberia or bust

Some people believed that the transatlantic cable would never work. They wanted to run cables north from California, through Canada and Russian America (later called Alaska, when it was bought by the U.S. government in 1867), and across the Bering Strait to connect with Russia and the rest of the world. Western Union thought this idea made good sense, and they chose three teams of men to build the line: one in Canada; one in Russian America; and one in Siberia, a part of northern Russia. When the finished lines were joined, they would link the United States and Russia.

Building the system was not easy, especially in Siberia. Winter brought bitter cold and only four hours of sunlight a day. In summer, the ground was so soggy from melting snow that they could not put up poles. Still, the determined men kept working.

When the men in Canada and Russian America heard that the transatlantic cable was laid and worked, they stopped building and went home. But the men in Siberia were cut off from the world. They kept working and did not find out that they were wasting their time until 1867, about a year after the cable was laid in the Atlantic.

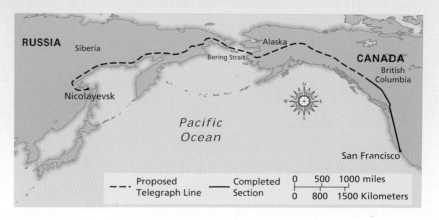

The News Wire

As the **telegraph** system grew, news began to spread quickly around the world. News that used to take days, weeks, or months to get from one place to another now took just a few hours or a few minutes.

Before the transatlantic cable was laid, newspaper reporters were so determined to get the news before their competitors that they sent reporters to meet ships arriving in New York's harbor. The reporters would get the news from the ships and race back to their offices to write news stories.

In 1848, several newspaper **publishers** met to discuss forming a **cooperative.** They called their group The Associated Press, or the AP. The purpose of the cooperative was to share news stories as information arrived. The Associated Press started with six of the most important newspapers in New York. It quickly grew to include reporters in Boston, Philadelphia, and Washington, D.C., as well as in Nova Scotia, Canada. The Canadian **correspondent** there, Daniel Craig, would meet ships that arrived from Europe and get news from them. Then he would use **Morse code** to telegraph the stories to the rest of the AP members. The AP covered the Civil War and President Lincoln's **assassination** in 1865, sending news stories by telegraph to member cities. In 1875, the group rented its own telegraph wire between New York, Philadelphia, Baltimore, and Washington, D.C. Today, the AP is the largest news **agency** in the world.

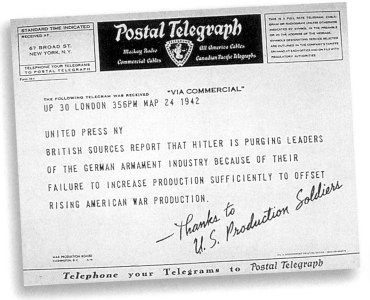

During World War II, many important messages were sent by **telegram** by foreign war correspondents to newspapers back home.

A similar group started in Paris in 1849. A man named Paul Julius Reuter used pigeons and **telegraphy** to send messages about the **stock market** around Europe. In 1851, he moved to London and established Reuter's Telegram Company. He kept Europeans aware of what was going on in the stock market by sending messages by telegraph from London to Paris. Soon his agency started including other kinds of news as well. In 1865, the agency was the first in Europe to spread the news of President Lincoln's assassination. After undersea cables were laid around the world, Reuters began to send stories to Asia and South America. Like the AP, Reuters is a popular news agency that continues to send stories over computer wires.

News agencies like Reuters and The Associated Press used the telegraph system to spread news quickly during World War II.

Wiring War

As the world became wired for the **telegraph,** people thought peace was at hand. Many believed that as people got closer and could communicate more quickly, they would get along better. War would be a thing of the past.

They were wrong. War continued, as it always had. The telegraph didn't create peace, but it did help armies to communicate with one another and to plan their moves.

The telegraph's first wartime use was in the Crimean War in Europe (1853–1856), although it was not widely used. During the American Civil War, though, the army used the telegraph often. A division of the U.S. Army called the Signal Corps made portable telegraph stations by placing telegraphs, wires, and poles on wagons. When a commander needed to get in touch with someone, the Signal Corps quickly set up the system and attached it to the nearest telegraph line. General Grant, the head of the Union army— the army of the northern states—often used code words in his **telegrams** in case the Confederate, or southern, army stole them. Two of the words he used were "Venus" for "colonel" and "Adam" for "U.S. president."

President Abraham Lincoln was the first U.S. president to rely on the telegraph. During the Civil War, he would walk to the War Department to check on the progress of the war. Reports came into the department several times a day by telegraph from Union army **telegraphers**. Lincoln didn't know **Morse code,** but he waited until the War Department telegraphers wrote up the reports, and then eagerly read them.

This photograph was taken during the Civil War and shows the telegraph station used by General Grant. Grant used **telegraphy** to give orders to hundreds of thousands of men during the Civil War.

These men are sending messages by telegraph during World War I. Use of the telegraph and the telephone were common then. However, wireless radiotelegraph systems became more popular because there were no wires that could be cut or damaged during battle.

The U.S. Army used Morse code in other ways as well. One system was called the **heliograph.** It was made of two mirrors that reflected the light of the sun, making bright flashes. A kind of shutter closed and opened in front of the mirrors. The operator would close the shutter quickly to make a dot and hold the shutter open for a longer time to make a dash. Because it needed sun, the heliograph was used mostly in the southwestern United States, where the sun often shines.

Another Morse code signaling system used torches. The operator put a kind of shutter or door in front of the torches and opened and closed the shutter to make dots and dashes.

The telegraph was also used during World War I, which was fought in Europe from 1914 to 1918. The army usually used wireless **radiotelegraph** systems during this war. The U.S. Army Signal Corps built many telegraph offices in Europe for U.S. soldiers to use. By that time, though, the army was also using telephones to communicate.

The Telegraph and the Railroad

In 1861, **telegraph** lines reached across the United States from coast to coast. In 1869, another first occurred when railroad lines linked both coasts. On May 10 of that year, the railroad's final spike—made of gold especially for the occasion—was driven into the ground in Promontory Point, Utah. Governor Leland Stanford of California lifted the hammer and missed, but the local telegraph operator, W. N. Shilling, had already started tapping out the message in **Morse code.** Stanford hit the spike on his next try, and the railroad was completed.

It took six-and-a-half years to complete the first transcontinental railroad, which spanned 1,800 miles (2,900 kilometers) across the United States.

People across the country waited anxiously for the news. Shilling tapped out "Done" in Morse code: — • • — — — — — • •. People cheered from San Francisco to Boston. Now the country was connected not only by telegraph, but also by train. What a wonderful age they lived in!

Even in the telegraph's early days, it had been closely linked to the railroad. Most city railroad stations had a telegraph office, and telegraph lines often ran alongside train tracks. Telegraph operators could warn train engineers of problems along the route or pass along important information. Trains ran smoothly because they could receive messages from up and down the tracks.

Telegraph poles and wires are visible in this photo next to railroad tracks. The telegraph system helped trains run more smoothly with fewer accidents.

Train passengers often used the telegraph, too. They could send messages to their loved ones back home or to the people they were traveling to see.

Sometimes robbers hopped onto trains at stations or when the trains were moving slowly. But they soon learned to cut the telegraph wires first. Otherwise, the operator could send a message and have police waiting at the next station!

Granville T. Woods

Granville T. Woods was an African American who was born in Ohio in 1856. He is sometimes compared to Thomas Edison because he invented so many things.

Woods's first job was repairing railroad equipment in a machine shop. He then worked as a railroad engineer. In 1878, Woods got a job as an engineer on a British steamer called the *Ironsides*. But because he was black, he was not allowed to do all the jobs he wanted to do. So in 1884, Woods and his brother started their own company, called Woods Railway Telegraph Company. They made telegraph and telephone products for use on railroads and in train stations.

Historians consider the synchronous multiplex railway telegraph to be Woods's most important invention. It allowed **telegraphers** and railroad operators to communicate with train engineers by Morse code while the trains were moving. This prevented a lot of accidents, because engineers could be warned about danger and stop the trains. Woods also invented air brakes and a **device** that allowed people to send telegraphs and telephone messages on the same wire.

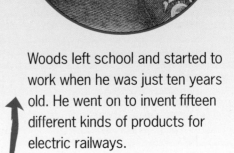

Woods left school and started to work when he was just ten years old. He went on to invent fifteen different kinds of products for electric railways.

Telegraph Operators

Telegraph operators, or **telegraphers**, felt they belonged to a special club. They knew a code that not many people knew, and they often talked to other telegraphers using this special code.

In the early days of **telegraphy**, people became telegraph operators often just by trying it out. They learned **Morse code** from other operators, then sat down and tried it to see how well they could do. Some people caught on quickly and did well, while others gave up and moved on to other jobs. Some got frustrated and quit because other operators on the line "salted," or teased them. When operators knew someone new was starting out, they would begin by sending messages at a slow rate. Then they would speed up, sending signals faster and faster, to see if the new telegrapher could keep up. Finally, they would let the new operator in on the joke.

Telegraphers had large contests to see who could tap out a message the fastest. They met in large halls. The **contestants** sat on a stage behind tables that held telegraph **devices.** Contestants were given part of a speech to tap out as quickly as they could, with as few mistakes as possible. The telegraphers in the audience would lean forward, listening closely to hear the words as they were being tapped. Good telegraph

These students attend class at a school for telegraphers in the early part of the 20th century. They receive messages in Morse code through the headsets they are wearing.

Telegraph companies in a major city like New York, where this telegrapher was photographed, may have had hundreds of employees.

operators could do 25 to 30 words per minute, but some contest winners managed to tap out 50 words in a minute. The audience would give outstanding telegraphers a **standing ovation.**

Good telegraphers usually went to work in large cities, where they could make more money than in small towns. Most small towns had a telegraph office, but the telegraphers there often worked only part-time.

When they were not busy, telegraphers would talk back and forth using their telegraph keys and Morse code. They often talked in a special kind of **shorthand** called Phillips code. Sometimes they even played checkers by Morse code! Telegraphers swore they could tell one operator from another by the way each tapped out Morse code.

Thomas Edison, telegraph operator

Before he invented the electric light bulb and many other things, Thomas Edison was a telegraph operator. In 1863, when Edison was sixteen years old, the local telegrapher in Port Huron, Michigan, went off to join the Military Telegraph Corps, sending and receiving messages for the Union army in the Civil War. Edison, who was fascinated by the telegraph and all its possibilities, replaced him. When he was not operating the telegraph key, he would read or go

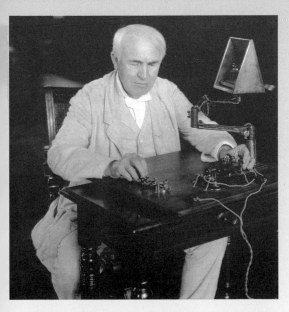

Edison was a telegraph operator when he was young. In this picture, an older Edison shows the photographer how he used to tap out Morse code.

down to the office basement and do experiments. Edison was a good telegrapher—he could tap out Morse code quickly. He always liked to work the night shift so he could do experiments during the day. Edison slept only a few hours each day, but sometimes he took catnaps while at work. Night shift operators had to signal every hour that they were awake and ready to send or receive messages. Edison managed to take short naps by rigging the telegraph device to automatically send "awake" messages every hour. He was caught, though, when he missed a message to stop a train, and the train nearly hit another train. When he discovered his mistake, he left that office. He continued to work as a telegrapher until he began inventing full-time. One of his inventions was a telegraph wire that could send or receive several messages at the same time.

Women and Morse Code

In the 1800s, few women worked. Those who did were often teachers or nurses. Many women stopped working as soon as they got married.

Women were also **telegraph** operators. The first woman to be a telegraph operator was probably Sarah G. Bagley. She worked in the telegraph office in Lowell, Massachusetts, in 1846.

Another women who worked as a operator during the early days of telegraph was Elizabeth Cogley. When she was in her late teens, she worked as a messenger for the Atlantic & Ohio Telegraph Company. In the 1850s, she became a telegraph operator for the Pennsylvania Railroad.

Sarah G. Bagley

Sarah G. Bagley did many important things in her lifetime. She lived in Lowell, Massachusetts, where there were many factories. In 1836, she went to work at a local cotton mill. A few years later, the owners of the mills in Lowell decided that workers needed to do more work for less money. Bagley formed a group called the Lowell Female Labor Reform Association. The group called for fewer hours—they wanted to work only ten hours a day—and better working conditions. She left her job at the mill, but continued to work with the association. She also wrote many articles about better working conditions for mill workers.

Then Sarah became interested in telegraph work. The telegraph came to Lowell in 1846, and she was hired to run the new telegraph office. In fact, records show that she was most likely the first woman to hold such a job. Sarah thought the telegraph was exciting, and she loved working as a telegraph operator. But some people in Lowell made fun of the idea that a woman could do such work. Sarah showed them they were wrong. She worked hard for only about $400 a year and paved the way for many women to become telegraph operators.

This telegraph office in Moscow, Russia, in the 1930s employed many women telegraph operators. It even had a nursery where employees' children could be taken care of during the day.

More women began to work as operators during the Civil War, between 1861 and 1865. More than half of the 2,000 men who were telegraph operators during that time joined the **military** as members of the Military Telegraph Corps. As they left, women replaced them. Many women continued to work after the war because their husbands had died in battle and they needed to support themselves and their families. But other women had to fight for their jobs when male operators came back from the war and wanted their old jobs back. Many of the men claimed that they could do a better job than the women, and the women argued back that they made few mistakes and could tap out **Morse code** as well as any man.

By the 1870s, more people began to accept women as telegraph operators. In New York, about three out of ten operators were women. Many of the pictures of telegraph offices drawn during that time show women operators. Few people were surprised to walk into a telegraph office and see a woman behind the counter.

Mystery women

Telegraph operators claimed that they could tell whether a man or a woman was tapping out a message. Men, they said, tapped firmly, while the touch of women was light. But a few men were fooled by this idea!

Telegraph operators rarely got the chance to meet, but when business was slow they would "talk" back and forth using Morse code. Once in a while the men were sure they were talking to another man because the operator's tapping was strong. When they found out a woman was on the other end of the line, they were embarrassed.

Sometimes romances blossomed between telegraph operators. After they had "talked" a while using Morse code, the operators would agree to meet somewhere. A few couples even married!

Wireless Telegraphy

In the late 1700s and early 1800s, scientists knew about the power of electricity, but they were not sure exactly what it could do. In 1864, James Clerk Maxwell, a science professor at Cambridge University in England, discovered that an electrical energy could travel in the form of waves. In 1888, another scientist, Heinrich Hertz, did a series of experiments with electricity. He found out that a spark of electricity would travel from one place to another, but he could get it to travel only five feet (1.5 meters).

Guglielmo Marconi, an Italian scientist, thought about what Maxwell and Hertz discovered. He tried a few of his own experiments using a **Morse key** to send electricity and another **device** that detected radio waves as a receiver. He managed to get sparks of electricity to travel 30 feet (9 meters). After improving the sender and hooking up an **aerial** to the receiver, he found that electricity could travel up to two miles (3.2 kilometers). Then he got it to travel across the English Channel! In 1899, Marconi put his **radiotelegraph** equipment on two American ships so they could send messages to New York about the progress of the America's Cup yacht race. The radiotelegraph worked fine, and people became excited about the possibilities of this new **technology.**

Guglielmo Marconi demonstrates the equipment he invented to send telegraph messages through the air by radio waves.

Cabot Tower on Signal Hill in the city of St. John's in Newfoundland, Canada, marks the spot where the first transatlantic wireless message from England was received.

In 1900, Marconi started a business called Marconi's Wireless **Telegraph** Company, Ltd. He hoped to show people that messages could be sent by telegraph not through wires, but through the air, using radio waves. Some people thought he was crazy, but he kept working at it. His plan was to send a message across the Atlantic Ocean by radiotelegraph.

In 1901, he set up everything he needed to send his transatlantic message. First, he built a sending station on the westernmost coast of England. Then he went to St. John's, Newfoundland, the easternmost point in North America. There, Marconi put up a large aerial and prepared to receive the message that would be tapped out in **Morse code** back in England. Wireless Morse signals sound like beeps instead of clicks. He could not hear the entire message, but he was able to get the Morse code signal for *S*.

Next, Marconi went aboard a ship, the *Philadelphia,* to do experiments. During the day he received messages from 700 miles (1,127 kilometers) away. At night, though, he could receive messages from 2,000 miles (3,219 kilometers) away. Marconi learned that this was because sunlight keeps the radio waves from going up far into the sky. Because there is no sunlight at night, the waves can go up higher and therefore travel farther.

Marconi and others continued to improve their senders and receivers. Because the wired telegraph worked so well on land, they concentrated on wireless **telegraphy** aboard ships. By 1914, all the armies and navies in the world used wireless telegraphy.

A Telegraph Office

A small-town or **rural telegraph** office usually had one operator. Some had two—one who worked during the day, and one who worked nights. The operator sat at a desk or table next to the telegraph **device**, listening for incoming messages or sending messages to other offices. A pile of blank forms was also on the desk. **Telegraphers** would record messages onto the forms.

Some telegraphers, particularly women, dressed up their offices with plants, curtains on the windows, and pictures. In the country, operators might bring their dogs or their babies along to work. When things were slow, telegraphers read books, chatted with other telegraphers by **Morse code**, knitted, or even took naps.

Before towns were wired with electricity, telegraphers had to take care of the **batteries** that powered the system. If the batteries didn't work, the telegraph didn't work. To take care of the batteries, telegraph operators had to clean them and add chemicals so they would

This small telegraph station in Alice Springs, Australia, was built in 1871 and linked the cities of Adelaide and Darwin.

At the height of **telegraphy**, telegraph offices in large cities were busy places.

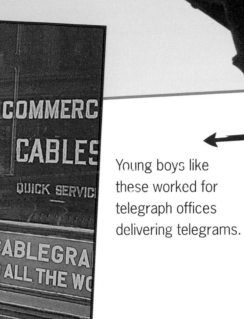

This old telegraph pole and wire stands at the site of an 1871 telegraph station in Arizona.

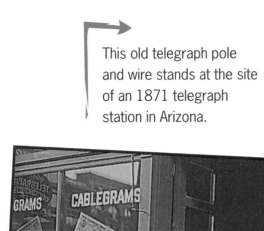

Young boys like these worked for telegraph offices delivering telegrams.

work properly. Some of the chemicals could be dangerous, so the operators had to work carefully.

Big-city telegraph offices were busy places. Twenty or more telegraphers could be working at the same time, and it took practice for telegraphers to hear their own instruments' "clicks" when other telegraphs were making noise beside them. In some offices, telegraphers put **telegrams** into **pneumatic tubes** similar to the ones used today at bank drive-in lanes. The telegrams went through the tubes to another room, where they were given to messenger boys who delivered the telegrams on foot or by bicycle.

Using Morse Code

Morse code does not have to be tapped out with a **telegraph** key. People all over the world have used it many different ways. Some people have used flashlights to send messages. Others have used their eyelids to blink messages in Morse code.

An American soldier in **Bosnia** in the mid-1990s taught his fellow soldiers to use Morse code. While they were on guard duty, they stood about 500 feet (152 meters) away from each other. They used their flashlights to flash messages back and forth to each other and to their sergeant in his tent office.

Prisoners also use Morse code to talk with one another. During World War II, Americans held in German prison camps communicated with one another by tapping out Morse code messages on pipes in their cells.

During the war in **Vietnam,** American soldier Jeremiah Denton was captured and held prisoner. Ten months later, the Vietnamese filmed an interview with him and sent it to be shown on American television. While Denton answered the reporter's questions, he blinked his eyes a certain

You can use a flashlight to send messages by Morse code to your friend down the street by shining a flashlight from a window that your friend can see.

Try sending messages in Morse code to a friend in the room next to you by tapping on the wall. A "dit" will sound like a quick knock, and a "dah" will sound like a slower knock.

way. When army officials looked more closely, they realized that he was blinking the word "torture" in Morse code, telling them that the Vietnamese were mistreating American prisoners of war.

Other prisoners tell the same kinds of stories. Today, some prisons have their own kind of Morse code, with **abbreviations** used just by people in those prisons.

If you and a friend learn Morse code, you can tap out messages back and forth or use flashlights to "flash" messages. You can even tap out a message into someone's hand when you do not want anyone to hear. Just tap quickly for dots and more slowly for dashes.

You can "speak" Morse code, too. A dot is a "dit." A dash is a "dah." So the letter *R* would sound like "dit dah dit." *T* is just "dah."

Hints for using Morse code

- When tapping or flashing Morse code, the dash ("dah") should be three times longer than the dot ("dit").
- Between each dit or dah, you should wait the length of one dit.
- Between letters, you should wait three dits.
- For example, the word "rat" looks like this in Morse code: • — • • — —. To send this word, you should tap or flash "dit (one silent dit) dah (one silent dit) dit (three silent dits), dit (one silent dit) dah (three silent dits), dah."
- Between words, pause for seven dits.
- You may not always have to use punctuation in Morse code—the person you are sending the message to may be able to understand when a sentence stops and starts. If you do not think the person will understand the message, however, use Morse punctuation!

Try these words in Morse code (you can use the alphabet on page 10):
Come   Please   Hello   Hamburger

Try writing or tapping out these sentences in Morse code:
- Please come to my party tomorrow.
- Did you do your homework?

These words and sentences can be found in Morse code on page 47.

Morse Code Today

Around the time World War II ended in 1945, people gradually stopped using the **telegraph.** Other inventions were making it easier to communicate. But the telegraph started it all—telephone, computers, e-mail, and even faxes.

Today, the only group of people who officially use **Morse code** are amateur radio (also called "ham" radio) operators. Thousands of people all over the world buy radio equipment and set it up in their homes. Many of them use Morse code to communicate. They call Morse code "CW," standing for "continuous waves." Operators who want to communicate this way have to pass a test and get a license to run their radio systems. Then they sign on and find someone to talk to in Morse code.

Around the world, amateur radio operators have been able to provide emergency communication in areas that have been struck by floods, fires, hurricanes, or other natural disasters. They have kept in contact with emergency services until regular communications have been fixed.

Today, there are 675,000 ham radio operators in the United States, and 2.5 million around the world. If you would like to get your amateur radio license, contact the American Radio Relay League in Newington, Connecticut.

Many people use ham radios just for fun. But they can also be used during natural disasters when telephones, televisions, and computers may not work.

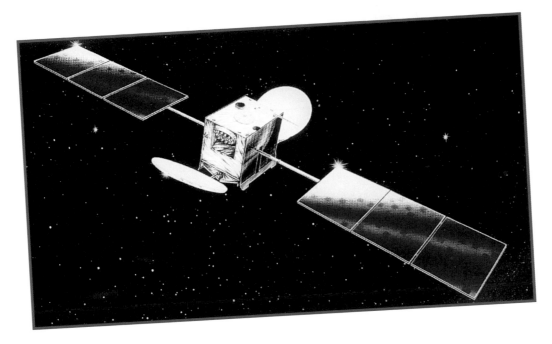

If a ship needs help, a GMDSS satellite like this one can quickly tell rescuers exactly where the ship is located.

As of February 1, 1999, Morse code—including the SOS **distress** signal that had been in use for so many years—was no longer the official way for people on ships to communicate. On that date, all passenger ships and cargo ships of a certain size were required by international law to use a **device** called the Global Maritime Distress and Safety System (GMDSS). This device uses radiocommunications equipment and is also linked to a **satellite** that can pinpoint the ship's position in the ocean so rescuers can find it quickly and bring help.

In this day and age Morse code does not have the same importance that it once did, but the people who use it today keep alive the tradition of an idea that changed the world. Morse code connected countries and people in a way they had never been connected before. Information and discoveries could be shared faster than ever. The world was never the same after its invention. What do you think will be the next invention to change the way the world communicates? Maybe you will be the one to invent it!

Appendix A:
The Phillips Code

Telegraphers used **abbreviations** like the ones below, called the Phillips code, when they talked with one another. Telegraphers who worked for news agencies, such as The Associated Press, also used abbreviations like these.

Awful . . . . .AWF	Could . . . . .CD	Girl . . . . .GL	Kindly . . . . . . .KDY	Month . . . . .MO
Automobile . . .AUMB	Chief . . . . .CF	Goodnight . . . . . .GNI	King . . . . .KG	Memory . . . . . .MMY
Across . . . . . . .ACX	Capital . . . . . . .CAP	Guess . . . . .GS	Keep . . . . .KP	Meet . . . . .MT
Afternoon . . . . .AFN			Know . . . . .KW	Matter . . . . . . .MTR
Around . . . . . . .ARJ	Danger . . . . . . .DNG	Handle . . . . . .HNDL	Knowing . . . . . .KWG	Million . . . . . .MYN
Ask . . . . .AX	Discuss . . . . . . .DS	Had . . . . .HD	Known . . . . . . .KN	Mystery . . . . . .MYS
	Disturb . . . . . . .DSB	Hope . . . . .HP		
Been . . . . .BN	Delivery . . . . . . .DLY	Here . . . . .HR	List . . . . .LST	Nothing . . . . . .MTG
Bring . . . . .BNG	Dollars . . . . . . .DOLS	High . . . . .HI	Listen . . . . . .LSN	Next . . . . .NX
By . . . . .BI	Do not . . . . . . .DT	Hold . . . . .HO	Laugh . . . . . . .LAF	Net . . . . .N
Began . . . . . . .BGA	Deserve . . . . . . .DSV	Holds . . . . . . .HOS	Language . . . . . .LAG	Name . . . . .NA
Begun . . . . . . .BGN	Days . . . . .DAS	Holding . . . . . .HOG	Last . . . . .LAS	Named . . . . . .NAD
Being . . . . .BG	Did . . . . .DD	Home . . . . . . .HOM	Life . . . . .LF	Names . . . . . .NAS
Believe . . . . . . .BV		His . . . . .HS	Long . . . . .LG	Neighbor . . . . . .NBR
Better . . . . . . .BTR	Every . . . . .EY	Hospital . . . . . .HSP	Longer . . . . . .LGR	Neighborhood . .NBH
Because . . . . . .BC	Equal . . . . .EQL	Happen . . . . . .HPN	Legal . . . . . . .LGL	Need . . . . .ND
Birthday . . . . . .BDA	Examine . . . . . .EXM		Little . . . . .LIT	Natural . . . . . . .NL
By the . . . . .BIT	Examined . . . .EXMD		Like . . . . .LK	Naturally . . . . . .NLY
	Examining . . . .EXMG	Income . . . . . . .ICM	Large . . . . . . .LRJ	Normal . . . . . .NOR
Came . . . . .CA	Excuse . . . . . . .EXQ	Instruct . . . . . . .INX	Learn . . . . . . .LRN	Next week . . . . .NXK
Close . . . . .CLO	Expect . . . . . . .EXK	Instructed . . . .INXD	Letter . . . . . .LTR	Never . . . . .NV
Chance . . . . . . .CNC		Instructing . . .INXG	Look . . . . .LUK	News . . . . .NUS
Come . . . . .CM	Fight . . . . .FHT	Instruction . . .INXN	Leave LV	Nearly . . . . . .NRY
Call CL	Fourth of July . . .FOJ	Illustrate . . . . . . .ILT	Leaves . . . . . .LVS	Night . . . . .NI
Called . . . . . . .CLD	For . . . . .FO	Immediately . . . . .IM		Notice . . . . . . .NTC
Closed . . . . . .CLOD	Favorite . . . . . .FVT	Improve . . . . . . .IP	Many . . . . . . .MNY	
Closing . . . . . .CLOG	Follow . . . . .FW	Impose . . . . . . .IPO	Most . . . . .MS	Order . . . . .OD
Closes . . . . . .CLOS	Fixing . . . . . . .FXG	Invade . . . . . . .IVA	Move . . . . .MV	Offer . . . . .OFR
Clear . . . . .CLR	Freeze . . . . .FZ	Invite . . . . . . .IVT	Must . . . . . . .MST	Office . . . . . . .OFS
Company . . . . . .CO	Frozen . . . . . . .FZN	Investigate . . . . .IVG	More . . . . .M	Organize . . . . . .OG
Charge . . . . . .CHG	Few . . . . .FU	It was . . . . .IW	Made . . . . .MD	Organized . . . . .OGD
Charged . . . .CHGD	Facts . . . . .FAX	It is IX	Middle . . . . . .MDL	Organizes . . . .OGS
Charging . . . .CHGG	First . . . . .FS	In view IV	Manage . . . . . .MG	Original . . . . . .OGL
Charges . . . .CHGS	Famous . . . . . .FMX		Managed . . . . .MGD	Object . . . . .OJ
City . . . . .CTY		Just . . . . .JS	Managing . . . .MGG	Omit . . . . .OM
Connect . . . . . . .CT	Give . . . . .GV	Judge . . . . .JG	Manager . . . . . .MGR	Omits . . . . . . .OMS
Care . . . . .CR	Giving . . . . . . .GVG	Jury . . . . .JU	Minute . . . . . .MIN	Omitted . . . . .OMD
Cares . . . . . . .CRS	Gave . . . . .GA	Jewelry . . . . . .JWY	Might . . . . . . .MIT	Occupy . . . . . . .OQ
Cared . . . . . . .CRD	Going . . . . .GG	Joint . . . . .JT	Make . . . . .MK	Occupied . . . . .OQD
Careful . . . . . .CFL	Gone . . . . .GN	Join . . . . .JN	Mail . . . . .ML	Occupying . . . .OQG
Celebration . . .CBN	Group . . . . .GP	Joined . . . . . .JND	Morning . . . . . .MNG	Occupation . . .OQN
Celebrity . . . . .CBY	Groups . . . . . .GPS		Modern . . . . . .MOD	Oppose . . . . . . .OS
Cancel CCL	Ground . . . . . . .GR	Kind . . . . .KD	Money . . . . . .MON	Opposes . . . . . .OSS

42

Opposing	OSG
Opposite	OST
Other	OTR
Our	OU
Otherwise	OWZ
Over	OV
Of	O
Of a	OA
On account of	OAC
Obtain	OB
Obtains	OBS
Obtained	OBD
Obtaining	OBG
O'clock	OC
Occur	OCU
Occurred	OCUD
Occurring	OCUG
Photograph	FGH
Paper	PAP
Probably	PBY
Problem	PBM
Proceed	PCD
Purchase	PCH
Paid	PD
Produce	PDU
People	PEO
Pieces	PCS
Prefer	PF
Preference	PFC
Perfect	PFT
Progress	PG
Paragraph	PGH
Program	PGM
Perhaps	PH
Prohibit	PHB
Project	PJT
Package	PKJ
Please	PL
Permit	PMT
Point	PNT
Possible	POS
Prepare	PPR
Proper	PRP
Part	PRT
Pass	PS
Passage	PSJ
Passes	PSS
Person	PSN
Public	PU
Purpose	PUR
Provide	PVI
Prevent	PVNT
Price	PX
Prices	PXS
Previous	PVX
Power	PW
Protect	PXT
Prize	PZ

Quick	QK
Quickly	QKY
Quite	QT
Quiet	QU
Quietly	QUY
Question	QSN
Quarter	QR
Raise	RA
Receive	RC
Received	RCD
Receiving	RCG
Read	RD
Reading	RDG
Reader	RDR
Reads	RDS
Radio	RDO
Repeat	REPT
Repeating	REPG
Refer	RF
Refuse	RFU
Regular	RG
Regard	RGD
Reach	RH
Right	RHT
Reject	RJ
Relief	RLF
Really	RLY
Realize	RLZ
Remain	RM
Remaining	RMG
Return	RTN
Receipt	RCT
Remove	RV
Removes	RVS
River	RVR
Review	RVU
Reward	RWD
Recommend	RX
Railway	RY
Result	RZ
Soon as Possible	SAP
Submit	SBM
Submitted	SBMD
Scare	SCA
Subscribe	SCB
Subscription	SCN
School	SCL
Season	SZN
Should	SD
Sudden	SDN
Said	SED
Saying	SEG
Says	SES
Seen	SEN
Satisfy	SFY
Satisfactory	SFY
Similar	SIM

Subject	SJ
Success	SK
Succeed	SKD
Schedule	SKJ
Self	SLF
Some	SM
Small	SMA
Somebody	SMB
Something	SMG
Sometime	STI
Soon	SN
Since	SNC
Send	SND
Sooner	SNR
Spoke	SPK
Spoken	SPKN
Special	SPL
Suppose	SPO
Speaker	SPQR
Serious	SRX
Strong	STG
Stronger	STGR
Steady	STY
Sure	SU
Suggest	SUG
Service	SVC
Serve	SVE
Season	SZN
The	T
Than	TAN
Trouble	TBL
Touch	TCH
Trade	TDE
Today	TDY
Territory	TEY
Traffic	TFK
Transfer	TFR
Thing	TG
Telegraph	TGH
Telegraphy	TGY
Those	TH
Thanks	TNX
Through	THRU
Though	THO
Thick	THQ
Their	THR
Time	TI
Take	TK
Taking	TKG
Taken	TKN
Them	TM
Temperature	TEM
Transmit	TMT
Then	TN
Think	TNK
Telephone	TPH
Transportation	TPN
There	TR

Typewriter	TPW
These	TSE
This	TS
That	TT
Toward	TWD
They	TY
Uncertain	UNC
Urgent	UGT
Understand	UK
Understanding	UKG
Unknown	UKN
Usual	UL
Until	UN
Under	UND
Unless	UNL
Unusual	UNU
Unable	UNA
Upon	UPN
Useful	USF
Utilize	UTZ
Value	VAL
Variety	VAY
Valuable	VB
Verify	VF
Vanish	VNQ
Vote	VO
Visible	VSB
Visit	VST
View	VU
Very	VY
With	W
Water	WAT
Welcome	WC
Would	WD
Wonderful	WDF
Weather	WEA
Weak	WEK
Wrong	WG
Weigh	WGH
Weight	WGT
Worse	WUS
Which	WH
While	WHI
Whole	WHL
Will	WI
Wound	WJ
Week	WK
Well	WL
When	WN
Who	WO
Whose	WOS
Were	WR
Word	WRD
Why	WY
Worth	WRH
Write	WRI

Wrote	WRO
Written	WRN
Was	WS
Work	WRK
What	WT
Wait	WX
Exact	XAC
Excite	XC
Extinguish	XGH
Exhaust	XH
Explain	XJ
Excel	XL
Excellent	XLT
Extreme	XM
Export	XPT
Export	XPT
Exist	XS
Exclude	XU
Exclusive	XUV
Year	Y
Yesterday	YA
Yesterday Morning	YAM
Yesterday Afternoon	YAP
Yesterday Evening	YAV
Years old	YO
And	&
That the	5
That is	7
Where	4
January	F
February	G
March	H
April	J
May	K
June	M
July	N
August	Q
September	U
October	V
November	X
December	Z
Monday	MDA
Tuesday	TUY
Wednesday	WDA
Thursday	THD
Friday	FRI
Saturday	SATY
Sunday	SDY

Appendix B: American Morse Code

American **Morse code** is sometimes called "Landline" code because it was used only by telegraphers who sent messages from one place on land to another. In 1865, many countries around the world decided to use another form of Morse code called International Morse code, which is still used today by ham radio operators.

A	•—	N	—•	0	——————
B	—•••	O	• •	1	•—•—•
C	•• •	P	•••••	2	••—••
D	—••	Q	••—•	3	•••—•
E	•	R	• ••	4	••••—
F	•—•	S	•••	5	———
G	——•	T	—	6	••••••
H	••••	U	••—	7	——••
I	••	V	•••—	8	—••••
J	—•—•	W	•——	9	—••—•
K	—•—	X	•—••	.	•——•••
L	————	Y	•• ••	,	•—•—
M	——	Z	••• •	?	—••—•

Glossary

abbreviation shortened form of a word

aerial tall, metal device used to receive radio waves

agency group that does business or performs a service

assassination quick, secret murder

barrier something that blocks the movement of something else

battery container called a *cell* that holds chemicals that make electrical energy

bison large, shaggy mammal that once lived in great numbers on the North American plains

Bosnia area in southern Europe; American soldiers went to Bosnia in 1995 when the Bosnians were fighting the Serbians. Serbia is a part of Yugoslavia.

chemistry science of what substances are made of and how they change

code message in which a word, phrase, letter, or other symbol replaces an entire message

coil number of turns of wire around a center, such as a spool

Congress U.S. governing body that makes and changes laws and decides how to spend government money; the U.S. Senate and the House of Representatives make up the U.S. Congress

contestant person who enters a contest

cooperative group of people or businesses who join together to share a service

correspondent person who gathers news and sends it to a newspaper or other news organization

culture beliefs and behaviors of a particular group of people

device piece of equipment that has a specific purpose

distress emergency; trouble

electric current flow of electricity through a wire or other means

electromagnet magnet created by electric current flowing through a coil of wire

electromagnetism magnetism created by electrical current

heliograph telegraphic system that uses mirrors and the sun's rays to send Morse code signals

insulator something through which electricity cannot easily flow; telegraph wire was threaded through glass insulators at the top of telegraph poles

invest to give a business money hoping to make more money from the business's profits; person who invests is called an *investor*

magnet something that has a magnetic field

magnetism occurs in magnets and electric currents; something that has magnetism attracts iron and other magnets

magnetic field area around a magnet in which magnetism can be felt

military group formed to fight or protect, such as army or air force

Morse code system of dots and dashes used to send messages by telegraph

Morse key part of telegraph device that is raised or lowered to stop or start flow of electric current

mural large painting, often on a wall

pneumatic tube tube through which items are sent by movement started by a quick burst of air

portrait painting or drawing of a person, usually showing only the face

publisher person who makes sure a magazine, book, or newspaper is printed and sold

radiotelegraph telegraph that receives messages by radio waves instead of wires; also called wireless telegraphy

rural country; area where few people live

satellite machine that orbits Earth or another celestial body

semaphore something used to signal so that people can see it with a telescope or the naked eye; a semaphore usually has two arms

shorthand kind of writing that uses abbreviations for words

standing ovation given by audience at the end of an excellent performance; audience stands, claps, and cheers

stock market market where stock— shares in a particular company—is bought and sold

technology use of science and research to improve life

telegram written form of message sent by telegraph wires

telegraph device used to send messages over wires using code, usually Morse code; also refers to the action of sending messages over wires; the telegraph was used from the mid-1800s to the mid-1900s

telegrapher person who operates a telegraph

telegraphy using a telegraph device

territory piece of land belonging to a particular government; before the U.S. was completely divided into states, certain plots of land were territories

translate to change something from one language or code to another; telegraphers translated Morse code into the language of their country

transmit to send something from one place to another

Vietnam small country in Southeast Asia; the United States fought a war in Vietnam from 1955 to 1975

voltaic cell uses chemicals to create electric current; a voltaic cell is a kind of battery

More Books to Read

Kerby, Mona. *Samuel Morse.* New York: Franklin Watts, 1991.

Packard, Mary. *Morse Code.* New York: Nancy Hall, 2000.

Parker, Janice. *Messengers, Morse Code and Modems: The Science of Communication.* Austin, Tex.: Raintree Steck-Vaughn, 2000.

Places to Contact

American Radio Relay League
225 Main Street
Newington, CT 06111
Telephone: (860) 594-0200
Website: *http://www.arrl.org*

Navy Historical Center
Washington Navy Yard
805 Kidder Breese Street SE
Washington Navy Yard, D.C. 20374
Website: *http://www.history.navy.mil*

Correct Morse code translations for page 39:
come   _•_• ___ __ •
please   •__• •_•__•• • •_ ••• •
hello   •••• • •_•• •_•• ___
hamburger •••• •_ __ _••• •_ •_• __• • •_•

Please come to my party tomorrow.
•_•__• •_•• •_••• • _•_• ___ __ • _ ___ __
_•__ •_•_• •_•• _ _•_• _ ___ __ ___ •_• ••_
___ •__ •_•_•

Did you do your homework?
_•• •• _•• _•__ ___ ••_ _•• ___ _•__ ___ ••_
•_• •••• ___ __ • •__ ___ •_• _•_ ••_•_••

Index

Page Layout by Vicki Fischman
Photo research by Amor Montes de Oca
Printed and bound in the United States by Lake Book
Manufacturing, Inc.

07 06 05 04 03
10 9 8 7 6 5 4 3 2 1

Library of Congress Cataloging-in-Publication Data

Price Hossell, Karen, 1957-
  Morse code / Karen Price Hossell.
    p. cm. -- (Communicating)
Summary: An overview of the history, development, and use
of Morse code.
Includes bibliographical references and index.
  ISBN 1-58810-486-9 (HC), 1-58810-942-9 (Pbk.)
  1. Morse code. [1. Morse code.] I. Title. II. Series.
TK5265 .P75 2002
384.1'4--dc21

                    2002001685

Acknowledgments
The author and publishers are grateful to the following for
permission to reproduce copyright material:
Cover photograph courtesy of
Philip Gendreau/Bettman/Corbis
Illustrations shown throughout of telegraph device and maps
by John Fleck; pp. 2, 3, 20C, 29, 46, 47 Corbis; p. 4T Mike
Feeney/Trip; pp. 4B, 28 Underwood Photo Archives; pp. 5,
8BR, 16, 18, 19, 22, 24, 26, 27T, 37B, 41 Courtesy of
NARA/Tom Pantages; p. 6T Grantpix/Photo Researchers,
Inc.; p. 6B Tony Freeman/Trip; p. 7 Tom Pantages; p. 8T
Science Photo Library/Photo Researchers, Inc.; pp. 8BL,
35T, 35C The Granger Collection, NY; p. 9T Dorling
Kindersley Ltd.; p. 9B Sheila Terry/Science Photo
Library/Photo Researchers, Inc.; pp. 13, 31, 35B
Bettmann/Corbis; p. 14T LOC/Science Source/Photo
Researchers, Inc.; pp. 14B, 15 Library of Congress; p. 17
Dick James; p. 20T Bruce Iverson; pp. 23, 27B
AP/WideWorld Photos; pp. 25, 30, 32B, 34 Hulton-
Deutsch Collection/Corbis; p. 32T Steve Warble; p. 36T
Janet Pugh/Trip; p. 36B Underwood & Underwood/Corbis;
p. 37T Lowell Georgia/Corbis; p. 38T MAF/Visuals
Unlimited; p. 38B SW Productions/PhotoDisc; p. 40 H.
Rogers/Trip

Every effort has been made to contact copyright holders of
any material reproduced in this book. Any omissions will be
rectified in subsequent printings if notice is given to the
publisher.

Some words are shown in bold,
like this. You can find out
what they mean by looking in
the glossary.

Morse Code

KAREN PRICE HOSSELL

Heinemann Library